FROG'S POND

A Nature Story by David Stephen
Illustrated by Marjorie Blamey

COLLINS COLOUR CUBS

When Frog was born he didn't look in the least like a frog. He was a tadpole—a pollywiggle—a tiny creature with a black head and a thin, black, wiggly tail. He had hatched from a tiny black dot-like egg contained in the spawn which floated on the surface of the water. There were thousands of such eggs in the spawn, like currants in a pudding.

While the tadpoles grazed on the Algae, other pond creatures preyed on the tadpoles, and large numbers were eaten before they were more than a few days old. One of their great enemies was the ferocious water beetle, which killed them faster than a frog kills snails.

Birds also preyed on the helpless tadpoles. Almost every day the magpie from Woodmouse Lane came along and dabbled in the shallow water to catch them. He picked them out of the water, squeezed them in his beak, then swallowed them.

A pied wagtail also came to the pond to hunt, and now and again he would catch and eat a tadpole. This was easy for the wagtail, because he was used to paddling about in shallow water when he was hunting; but he didn't kill as many tadpoles as he could have done. He liked a variety of food and spent most of his time hunting along the water's edge, running this way and that, and constantly bobbing his tail.

Even when they were much bigger the
tadpoles were still preyed upon by water
beetles and their larvae, and the
larvae of the dragonfly.

But our Tadpole who-was-
to-become-a-frog managed
to escape from them all.
Although he still fed a
great deal on Algae he
was now hunting tiny
water creatures as well,
and was as much a hunter
as the water beetles and
dragonfly larvae that
preyed upon tadpoles.
That is to say he had
become a *Predator* as well
as a *Prey* species.

When he was a month old, he began to grow his hindlegs, but it was another fortnight before they were fully grown, complete with toes. Now he had a big appetite and sometimes even killed tadpoles smaller than himself.

Soon afterwards his forelegs
began to sprout. When they
had grown into real legs he
became more like a frog than
a tadpole, except that he
still had his tail.

Then he lost his tail too. But it didn't fall off, or wither off. It was absorbed into his body like an item of food. Many other tadpoles had also become real frogs, and one summer day, during a warm shower of rain, thousands of them left the water to begin their life on land. A big cat was crouched on the bank watching the migration of the little frogs.

But he wasn't hunting, so he didn't unsheath a claw at Frog, who hopped past not knowing how close to death he had been.

During the summer months, Frog spent all his time in ditches, long grass, and other wet places. But he didn't go back to the pond. He caught mites and plant lice and snails and other small crawly creatures. During the hottest part of the day he stayed in the shade, or in wet grass, because he felt distress when his moist skin was exposed to the sun for too long.

Once the weather became
cold Frog knew it was
time for him to hide
away for the Winter.
So he returned to the
pond and burrowed into
the mud under the bank
to hibernate. He was
now just under an inch
in length.

The noisy rooks were busy at their nests when Frog crawled from his muddy sleeping place the following spring. The frost had gone. It was a mild day with light showers of rain. Frog hopped along to Woodmouse Lane where he soon found enough food to satisfy his hunger. There were other young frogs there hunting under the hedges, and grown-up ones on their way to the pond to spawn. But Frog was still too young to join them.

Instead he stayed with the young frogs of his own age and spent the spring and summer in ditches, woods and other damp places, living a free, roving life. There was an abundance of food and he grew bigger and bigger.

He hunted beetles and flies and slugs and woodlice and caterpillars. Now and again he would catch and eat a small earthworm, but creatures like centipedes he ignored completely. These were carefree days and he was never in the same spot for long.

Frog caught flies with his tongue, in the same way as a chameleon does. His tongue rolled out to catch a fly, then rolled back in again with it trapped in the fold. He caught a lot of prey on grass stalks, and on the stems of hedgerow plants, by licking them off with his tongue. He did most of his hunting crawling about, or sitting still—waiting.

On many days much of his prey consisted
of small snails and beetles, which he
stuffed into his mouth and swallowed
with great relish. Quite often slugs
and snails looked far too big for him
to swallow, but he managed to gulp them
down. However, the really big ones were
too much for him, and when he found he
couldn't swallow them he left
them alone and hopped away to
look for a prey more suitable
to his size.

All the time he was growing bigger.
One day his skin split up the back
and he struggled out of it. But it
wasn't his real, coloured skin. What
he shed was its thin outer covering,
which had become too tight
for him. By the time he
was ready to hibernate
again he had grown to
a length of $1\frac{3}{4}$ inches.

Frog was three years old when he came out of hibernation for the third time, and now he travelled to the pond where he had been born. He was adult and ready to breed.

During the day the frogs croaked in chorus, especially when the sun was shining. When clouds hid the sun Frog liked to crouch on the lilypad for five or ten minutes at a time, resting or croaking. Many frogs died at this time—of exhaustion or old age. Some died ashore and some in the water. The bodies were gobbled up by rooks and crows in the daytime, and by hedgehogs, foxes and rats at night.

There were toads spawning in another part of the pond, where the water was deeper. In the water the two species kept mostly apart, and their paths seldom crossed. Even the toad tadpoles seldom ventured into the frogs' area. But once in a while there was a mix-up along the border between their territories.

Out of the water the frogs and toads
were more likely to meet. Early one
morning Frog came face to face with
a toad and they stared at each other
for a long time. Then the toad
crawled away and Frog leaped back
into the pond.

After a period of croaking, and resting, and plopping about, the frogs began to spawn, and before long great masses of jelly were afloat on the pond. Children came to the pond with small buckets or glass jars and collected spawn to take home, or to school, where they could watch the tadpoles hatching out. Some thoughtless children gathered spawn and threw it on the ground, thus destroying thousands of eggs that would have become tadpoles.

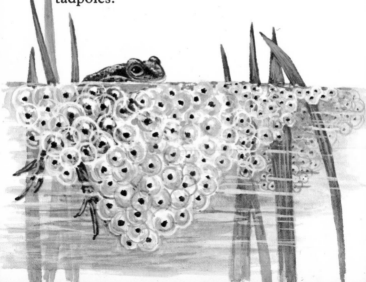

Many animals like to eat frogs, and
because so many frogs gather together
at spawning time the hunters find
them an easy prey. One of the great
frog hunters was the heron. He would
stand in the water for long periods,
like a statue, and when a frog came
within reach he would stab down with
his beak, snatch it, and walk ashore
with it to eat it.

At dusk, and during the night, when the frogs were asleep or resting, a hedgehog came along to the pond to hunt frogs— even in the water. If he couldn't catch one ashore he thought nothing of swimming around in the shallows to seek them. Then there was the owl from Woodmouse Lane, who often flew across the pond at night. If he spied a frog hopping about on land he would swoop down upon it and try to snatch it in his talons.

One day a carrion crow tried to catch
Frog when he was ashore. But Frog
escaped by taking a great leap and
diving into the water with a *plop*.
Another frog, resting in the shallows
with its head out of the water,
was snapped up by the crow instead.

The first frogs to mate and spawn
left the water first. Frog watched
many of them go but was not yet
ready to leave himself. Herons
killed some of the departing frogs,
while others fell a prey to rats.

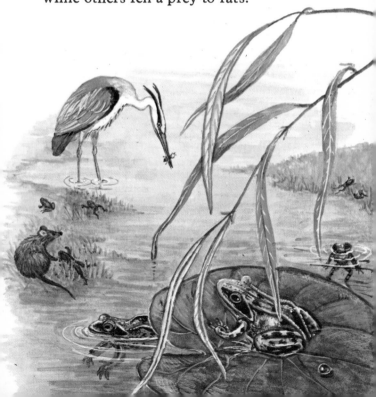

One night, when Frog was ashore, his
life almost came to an end when a
hedgehog snapped at him and caught him
by a hindfoot. Frog leaped about madly
but could not escape the hedgehog's
grip. He mewed in despair—a cry like
the faintest mewing of a small kitten,
and one rarely heard by human ears.
The hedgehog snapped his teeth into the
frog's foot, and it is very likely he
would have begun to eat Frog alive if
there hadn't been an interruption.

Suddenly the hedgehog released his grip
and curled into a defensive ball.
Realising he was free, Frog leaped madly
into the water. A fox appeared and began
to roll the coiled hedgehog about with a
forepaw. So Frog lived. But the
hedgehog died.

Frog's foot bled a little, but it wasn't seriously damaged, and for a few days he didn't leave the water. When he did hop ashore the first thing he met was the Jack Russell terrier from the farm, out for a romp. Being a Jack Russell, the terrier couldn't resist rushing at Frog to catch him. But he wasn't quite fast enough with his pounce, and when his forepaws touched the ground Frog had already leaped wildly into the air to escape him.

The terrier, determined to catch Frog,
leaped up snapping his jaws. But by
then Frog was on the way down again.
The dog tried many times to catch him,
but Frog was always down when the
terrier was up, and up when he was
down. In the end Frog escaped into
the water, saved by his agility. For
a long time afterwards, he floated in
deep water with only his head showing.
Then he crawled on to his lilypad to
recover his wits.

Nearby he saw a male stickleback guarding his nest from the female who wanted to eat the eggs she had just laid in it.

Next evening Frog left the pond, still slightly crippled, but able to hop and leap, and before morning he had eaten fifteen snails. During the day he hid in a cool, mossy ditch, out of the heat of the sun. In the moist dusk he went hunting again, his appetite as big as ever.

He was feeding beside a small pool when
a stoat came bounding along to pounce on
him, but Frog leaped from under its paws
and dived into the deep water to safety.
The stoat hissed in disappointment, but
went on its way, knowing it had no hope
of catching Frog in the water.

Frog had now no special home, so he was free to move about as he pleased. One night he was hunting spiders and moths in Squirrel Wood when he came face to face with a woodcock on her nest. The bird, who was sitting on four eggs, didn't move, even when Frog bumped his nose against her feathers. She wasn't in the least afraid of him, and if he had been smaller, she might even have eaten him.

In Squirrel Wood a pair of long-eared
owls had young in a hole under a tree
root. Frog hopped right into the nest
one night but luckily he was out of it
again, on the other side of the tree
root, when one of the owls flew in with
prey. The owl didn't see him; otherwise
Frog might have finished up as prey for
the owlets.

Frog found a lot of his food among the clover in a field where cows were grazing. Sometimes he would hop right up to a cow when she was chewing the cud, but the good-natured animal paid no attention to him.

Frog liked Woodmouse Lane
very much and spent a lot of
time there. Although the lane was
usually quiet it had its dangers, and
one night Frog was caught in the head-
lamps of a car approaching Cock Robin's
Garden. Frog squatted down as the car
came on, and the wheels passed on either
side of him, so he wasn't injured.

Near the farm duck-pond he was chased by hungry ducks but managed to escape by diving into a woodpile.

The ducks really frightened him, so he
left the farmyard and hopped back along
Woodmouse Lane, cramming himself with
slugs and snails which he stuffed into
his wide mouth with his forefeet. For
the next two days he hunted beetles and
caterpillars in Cock Robin's Garden.

Thus Frog lived his free, wandering
life, hunting in Cock Robin's Garden,
along Woodmouse Lane, and in Squirrel
Wood. There was plenty of food so he
continued to grow and by the autumn
he had reached his full size. When
the weather became too cold for him
he set off for the pond to seek out
a place to hibernate. On the way he
met other frogs and joined up with
them. The frogs knew how to find the
pond which they recognised by smell.

The frogs dived into the water and for a day or two swam about lazily, as though very tired. Then one after another they sank to the bottom, where they began to burrow into the mud, stirring up ooze which clouded the water. Once the water had cleared again the frogs were all out of sight, secure in their blankets of mud. They were hibernating and would not come out again until the following March.

ISBN 0 00 123286 X